HISTORICAL (hysterical)

POETIC RIDDLES

IN **Rhythm n' Rhyme**
ALA JAZZ

JACK TAFOYA

authorHOUSE®

AuthorHouse™
1663 Liberty Drive
Bloomington, IN 47403
www.authorhouse.com
Phone: 1 (800) 839-8640

Published by AuthorHouse 11/09/2016

ISBN: 978-1-5049-8244-3 (sc)
ISBN: 978-1-5049-8245-0 (e)

Print information available on the last page.

<u>Books by Jack Tafoya</u>

How Numbers Control Your Life And Give Your Life Purpose   2007

How The English Language Controls The World   2009

Historical Poetic **RIDDLES in Rhythm n' Rhyme**   2016

Available online at <u>www.AuthorHouse.com</u>

and **Amazon.com**

TABLE OF CONTENTS

PERSONAL POETRY

LOVE POEMS

PREFACE

The **Historical Poems** in this book were composed over a period of years from 1980 to 2004. The **Personal Poems** were composed in 1982 except for a song **A Summer Affair** composed by the author and dedicated to the author's soon-to-be model/wife from Holland. The song was first performed by the author in the Aruba Caribbean Hotel *Bally Bar* Lounge in Aruba, Netherlands Antilles where he headlined with his musical group **The Internationals** in 1962.

The **Historical Poems** may seem cynical to some readers, but they are based on researched facts and clues to information that came to the author in **visions** through the years. The Historical Poems are basically a synopsis of all the material in the authors' two previously published books HOW NUMBERS CONTROL YOUR LIFE AND GIVE YOU LIFE PURPOSE 2007 and HOW THE ENGLISH LANGUAGE CONTROLS THE WORLD 2009.

INTRODUCTION

By Jack Tafoya

The following poetry is a synopsis of my two published books. My research for this book reaches back to a time when world domination by cold white men was in its first planning stages I prophetically called The Ice Plan Code. After years of research, I finally realized The Ice Plan was actually based on "malice aforethought (*mal, L. bad ice*)." It took me years to recognize how the **plan** evolved step by step through time into a **plot**, then to a **scheme**, to a **conspiracy**, and finally being 'dictated' by a universal language called **English**, which people would naturally construe and accept as a "**benevolent dictator**," but a dictator never-the-less called the **Dictionary**. Who would imagine that the dictionary could be the instrument (tool), and words would be the weapons to control masses of humanity?

Ask yourself "who questions the dictionary?" The dictionary is the number one best-seller in the world, and its number two best-selling partner is the King James BIBLE, both from England our 'mother country'. Well, my book questions the Dictionary as you will experience reading the following poems "Pair a Balls From Paradise" and "Cold Man With a Plan". My latest book "How The English Language Controls The World" shows precisely **how** it was done.

Pair a Balls from Paradice: Parody or Paradox?
Composed in 1985

You the reader have a spelled-out option of viewing the creation of this first poem as a parody or a paradox even though some individuals who know my works have suggested it could become a paradigm. The choice of selecting the title Historical (Hysterical) Poetic **RIDDLES in Rhythm n' Rhyme -** with a touch of humor - was a natural instinct to convey my perceptions of controversial, very serious material throughout the Historical Poetry as well as a portion of the **Personal Poetry.**

I was a jazz musician/vocalist most of my younger life - late 1940s, 50s and 60s, then a jazz TV producer/host, live concert and radio host, and record producer in NYC in the 1970s. I wrote the poetic Riddles in the late 90s with words that requires the reader to search for his own perception of the word-meanings….like jazz which is improvisational. Rhyme and Time sets the rhythmic mood, like Jazz musical notes.

I can only assume that by now you have figured out that **Pair a Balls** (Old and New Testes - Testaments) is a play on the word Parables, and **From Paradise** is "from above". Even though you may consider yourself a religious person, keep an open mind and I trust you will find this poem enlightening and entertaining as well as making a point.

You decide if this is a **Parody** *or a* **Paradox,** *and, just in case you are unaware or cannot recall, here are the definitions.*

Parody - Fr. L. Gr. Paroidia. Para - beside + oide, song. *A musical or literary composition imitating the styles of some other work or of a writer or composer, but treating a serious subject in a nonsensical or humorous manner. To make a parody of.*

Paradox - Fr. L. Gr. < para - beyond + doxa, opinion <dokein - to think> *A statement that seems contradictory, absurd, etc. but may be true in fact. A person or thing seeming inconsistent and contradictory.* Pair a Balls From Paradice is "a play on words".

PAIR A BALLS FROM PARADICE

Try taking in this poetry with an open mind;
In the contents I am confident you will find
information both searching and bold, about two testis, one
NEW and one OLD.

And if you're thinking "this guy Jack can't be serious."
Be assured, I am not delirious.
Read it through and maybe one day
you will realize I had something to say;

How we've been hooked on theology far too long,
teaching "**right is right**" leaving **left** to be **wrong**.
The dictionary dictating white as **good**, black as **bad**.
Why can't we face it, we have been had.

Of the many books I read and learned very well,
the Bible and Dictionary are the world's biggest sell.
The Bible introduced a **confounding language** by man,
while the Dictionary dictates its meaning by plan.

It took years to realize how the Bible called **The Word,**
makes the Dictionary essential for one to be heard.
Confounding meanings; **wrong** and right / **left** and right.
In the Dictionary - directions; in the Bible **dark** and light.

These two books - the main ideological forces
are from the same Roman/Judeo Anglican sources.
These two infamous books that go hand-in-hand,
are both best sellers all through the land.

Reli on **The Word** for heaven and/or hell;
Depend on the **Dictionary** to use **The Word** well.
One book serves the other, the other serves the One!
This third book to uncover what is being done.

It is said "what is done is done, you can't change the past".
The past **is** the past; but for the future we must learn very fast!
We are busy buying and selling everything we see,
but saving little for what will eventually be.

We still have enough sustenance on planet earth,
but the Dog in man is dogging it to **d**earth.
Material things; of late I've collected very little.
Between **right** and **left,** I'm in the middle.

Knowledge and understanding "I have" it's been said.
The dog-part in me is buried and I know it is dead!
It is now time to speak my mind and heart,
so that **you the people** may get a new start.

I feel the pain of the mom called Virgin Mary
losing a son she was **destined** to carry.
I also understand the desperate plight
of the ever fleeing Diaspora Semite.

American Indians are colo**red**, not black,
so, why are they also flat on their back?
I had disbelief about the black slave
until I saw how white men behave.

The native in me knows the grueling fight
of the western Indians in constant flight.
The **left** arm **din** makes eating Buffalo a sin
while the **right** arm **white** gets everything in sight.

Imagine! THE GOOD SHIP JESUS sanctioned by thePope,
was **first** to rob the black African slave of his hope.
Now "black on black crime" is working on time! **Frustration**
was the **bet** when the script was set.

Kike! Spic! Nigger! Is there a name even bigger?
How about **savage**, the white man's **ravage**?
The native in me heard white man's "forked tongue"
while I was searching and still very young.

In my youth it made me feel angry and sad,
when I read "white lies are OK, red and black bad".
I've never heard of a 'yellow lie', but as I speak,
I'm aware we've all heard of a "yellow streak."

My Spanish-born father who now is in heaven
begot six boys and six girls; my number is seven.
His Spanish, **her** Irish, and ish means **is h**ell.
Don't mess with mom's Irish! I remember that well!

I chose neither moms' Ir**ish,** nor dads' Span**ish**.
Neither one-nor- the-other was my wish.
My father and mother were programmed **to be**,
A righteous program **to be** reprogrammed on me.

I went from the **left** Spanish-Catholic frying-pan,
to the **right** Irish-Protestant hell-fire man.
My mother kept repeating, (bless her soul)
"sing praise to The Lord to make you whole."

I thought, "Me? Sing for this cruel **He** God
who dictated sternly **Don't spare the rod.**"
Sing for Lord Jesus made more sense,
but, it put me right back on the fence.

Fear and pain throughout the **Old** book,
and this, the **He** to whom I should look, or
Praying to "Virgin Mary, **mother** of God;"
when we all know she really carries the rod.

So, I slid-back away from the **fire**, back to the **pan**,
and looked to the New Teste for that savior man,
to save me from the Old Teste's God of Hellfire;
not from this Satanic Earth I've known as desire.

Religion was my test and I tried my best
to find the truth, but it required a sleuth.
All alone since in my ever-thinking quest;
permuting and writing with little or no rest.

I don't **believe** just because I'm told;
I'm not a lamb, not one of the fold.
I'm not a follower in the tail of the beast,
being drag-on(d) to the Saturnalia feast.

I'm Capricorn the Goat, first in the light.
I will not make Lambs with a **Kid** in sight.
I was a "seed" in the head of the Ram,
a Capricorn Goat, hardly a lamb.

The Goat is a leader who gets to the top,
while the lamb is a follower destined to flop.
Aries the Ram with a Ewe gets a Lamb,
while Capricorn the Goat gets a bastard Kid. 6

Abel the Lamb pleases God who "spares the rod"
While Kid Cain is kicked out without a doubt.
Mamas' boy Cain worked out in the rain.
Daddy's boy Abel brought lambs to the sacrifice table.

BILLY THE KID

Who's got **your** back Kid Billy?
Watch out for your so-called "friends".
There's Jack Kennedy, Marilyn Monroe
and Princess Diana who all met the same ends.

In a planned amnesty plot you'll be buried
next to your **real** dad who wasn't married.
They've got the moves down Garrett **Pat,**
tracking you to the ranch where Pete Maxwell's at.

Maxwell (House) Ranch-time where Pete was the master
who made Billy a William Bonney-born bastard.
Like Cain, they said "let's kill the bastard kid."
They tried and tried, and finally "**friend**" Pat Garrett did.

Billy, you'll have visitors of another kind.
Not like the ones you left behind.
Near the HAnger 18, "R" a NINE,
puts one right at Roswell House time.

ETs have been visiting you there
and I hope you make time to spare.
As the government does, don't pull out your gun;
The ETs who come here are **not likely to run.**

They were here on earth way back in biblical times,
but now they are leaving very few signs.
They are the God the Hebrews wrote about,
but now **right** and **left** leaves us with doubt.

Right God? Left God? It's hardly a riddle,
and there I am, stuck in the **Gaza** middle.
Your God? My God? Let's go to war!
My protestant God will win, cause "yours is a whore"!

Face it, if the problem is God, and who **He** chooses,
then for sure, one side wins and the other side loses.
He has already chosen claim both Arabs and Jews.
Then logically, everyone else is born to lose.

The End of Days? The religion battle is on,
but it won't matter when and if we're all gone.
Choosing sides makes it even worse,
in a religious desert war so diverse.

Are **they** who own The Kingdom of Heaven on Earth
chosen to inherit the Kingdom of Heaven by birth?
The Fabian Society who proposes a much better life,
or The Holy Roman Empire who would keep us in strife?

Is that **reality?** Not! There is only perception.
Is the God of The Bible man's conception,
or a **Plan** created with mal.**ice** aforethought?
Uncover the ICE PLAN, uncover the plot!

Like I keep saying, "The Truth **Lies** in Words."
Ask one of president Obama's new flocking
"ET CABINET BIRDS".

COLUMBUS SAILED THE OCEAN BLUE

The Vatican **plan**! Three Spanish ships would sail west!
Spain's Queen agreed, but the gold was her quest!
The Jesuits would gain; the western natives would lose.
They got suckered with Christen**dumb** and booze!

Spain's **Queen Bee** Isabella, Queen Pain-In-the 'S'.
The Vatican wanted native souls, but she could care less.
Columbus had an alien encounter; Magellan had one too.
Cotton Mather also saw the UFO light come out of the ocean blue.

The natives thought the white settlers came from the sky.
Columbus came posing as Jesus "to save them when they die."
The west was ass.ailed from the Spanish blue;
yet, there was another worldly event in 1492!

The Jew's were evicted from Spain! Who made a deal?
Repeat in your head; Africa - Spain - Israel, **Africa'S pain is real!**
England planned to give Israel back to the Jews,
in return for their Bible the **Anglers** planned to use.

With the dictionary as **God of The Words**
to gain Christian control as Anglican/alien birds.
Chrystals were taken from the ancient west
by the three Spanish ships that began the quest.

One ship returned home reporting the fix,
while two ships marked a spot in the deep six.
Bermuda try-angle-down equidistant force,
pulling the icecaps, you can **bet** on that horse.

Atlant**is** Bermud**is**, Cub**is**, a.ten **is** a one.
The **Azores**, (**B**), **C**anaries, the deed is done.
Searchers are now looking in the wrong place for a clue.
Miami, Bermuda and Puerto Rico will never do.

Two ABC triangles overlap for an amazing fit,
when the continents are back to before they split.
One, two, and three (**is**) A, B, and C.
Where-o-where can the **Atlantis Crystals** be?

Is is a ten, means the same ending again.
Aruba is due; ABC islands south for a clue.
There are three cardinal directions starting with N.E.W.
Four directions adding letter S. What happened to the other two?

They are **up** and **down** making the world go round.
Other-wise flat, said by those I am **that**!
SEA r CH! The Sea is God and who owns the sea?
H.M.S. Bounty, for royalty who claim **to be**

From the Gods - to be looked-up-to and praised.
Religious folks believe while I am amazed!
Why can't we see it, both plain and clear;
The Illuminati Bilderbergers create world fear.

The Trilateral bankers control **The Word,**
so that **we the people** cannot be heard.
They control the media and the TV news
to impose their political and philosophical views.

We are now barely surviving in this Age of Langu
Orwell predicted as Newspeak / Doublespeak.
The media masters have the masses by the tongue
so that **eating** and **speaking** becomes very bleak.

Wake up America! You are being used
by the King James Bible and Dictionary that are fused
as a giant Frankenstein Monster to control the world
for the Roman/Judeo Anglican/Ice-men playing God.

CAUSATION

Plant the seeds of things,the primal germs we teach.
Whence all creation around us came to be,
they warned us not to reach.   *Lucretius*

Not to reach is not to go, and not to go is not to grow.
So, go and grow and feel the rain,
and experience each cycles growing pain.

Creation is certainly not static,
but obviously not automatic.
Causation needs relation.
It takes two to seed creation.

Worlds come from world seeds.
The**os** and Gon**os** the master key.
From cosmos and gonos - **cosmogony**.
Creation can, and can.is **to be**!

Adam, Adamu as primordial man,
although one-half the celestial plan.
The extra rib, a bibliographical fib.
Takes two to make three; matter came **to be.**

Egyptian, Babylonian, Hindu mythology
benefits Hebrew, Greek, and Roman theology.
Woven into an Anglican Bible version;
Religionists of water immersion.

Intelligence and energy, together the cause;
Their seeds germinate to create motion.
Father and mother - celestial and terrestrial,
manifest a chaotic life in this great ocean.

Chaos, Cosm**os**, Gon**os** is The**os** - seven tied to three.
Numbers tied to **letters** are **powers** you don't see.
The logic of the **Monads** came from the **Gonads**;
the motivation of self-generation we came **to be.**

Letter R means **Is**, and letter Y is male.
The**o.R.y**; a concept, a plan, or a tale?
Using letters as food for thought,
when did their **plan** become a **plot**?

The pain of 'S' in the earth called O,
with Yin Yang force to make it go.
God is Mother G-7 and father D-4;
Cosmos and Gonos of pain-in-the-S more.

Genetic consciousness rising, but bound.
All that matter(s) holding it down.
Woman, the enemy of its progress
is truly epigenetic pain-in-the-S.

She fears truth and loves illusion;
resents change and escapes to religion.
Her child rates first, while He rates third;
propagation, security, and a sucker for the word.

Man created the word that he could be heard.
Declares "The Word is God, God is The Word"
Hence, man is The Word, "air in need of fire".
He controls her thinking **F,** leaving her with **ire.**

The '**if**' in l**if**e makes life an **if**;
if Ewe could see like Eye.
Your thinking - letter **F -** in his hands,
your life is now **man's lie**.

Thinking for yourself is not a crime,
faith should not be blind.
Stand up please! Get off your knees;
lambs are left behind.

Religion is narcotic; a habit of depend /rely.
Nuns wear the cat habit, Cat.holic do or die.
Dependence is an opiate drug that puts you on your knees;
It puts you in the habit of asking "give me please".

Asking God for everything will get you very little.
May as well spend your time playing **"Hey diddle diddle".**
Doing for others will get you what you earn;
so what more is there for you to finally learn?

In the Bible Book of Numbers **even** sons went to war,
but the bible never mentioned what the **odd** sons were for.
Two, four, six, eight, who do we appreciate?
Three, five, seven, nine; let's all have a good time!

Even dogs and odd cats are the sons of patriarchs.
The cats will stay and play…while the dog barks
and does it daddy's way.
Even Abel lost his life. Cain was **odd** and got a sister wife.

It proves that Numbers do exist,
so put **Numbers** on your priority list.
"God is a number" Pythagoras said,
and verily, verily, he got dead.

Jack said; "The truth **Lies** in words,"
so keep the **Numbers** in your head.
In Genesis; **Number the names** in lieu of dates of birth.
Cain, a nine; a zero sign, of a woman's worth.

Ab.**el.even**, a sacrificial **lamb**, who surely went to heaven.
Both be gone, now three is one, and Seth inherits number seven.
"Sefirot" seven and three is ten is one.
Mon.o.the.is.m! The deed is done!

A change of names for Abram and Sarai,
rewarded a **boy** plus **disc**.over.**y**.
Numbers and letters is a game they say;
a game of hide and seek.
Find the numbers in a name
and you'll get just a peek.

But numbers in a birth have worth;
more than in a name.
Birth-dates can't be changed like names;
the numbers stay the same.

In the bible myths of prophets old,
the Word was God; his name we're told.
Change your name to God and see,
if God is who you were meant to be.

Man created God as **The Word**
so that **He** could be **verily** heard.
Hence, man is The Word, air in need of fire.
He controls her thinking **F**, leaving her with **ire**.

Ire (in English) is anger, the anger of an Ire.land.
That name, land of ire, just happened, or was it planned?
"Sticks and stones break bones, but names are even worse.
It had to be a stupid asshole who wrote it in reverse.

If you were named Ur**anus** by your mother,
an asshole you'd be seen by any other.
You'd quickly change your name to Smith or Jones,
so no real assholes would break your bones.

Names can maim; words can kill,
but on them we depend.
To keep us above the animal world,
a life we can defend.

"Do **unto** others" translates "do **to** others";
an aggressive commandment it seems.
"Do **for** others" is much better;
it sounds and says just what it means.

An Abyss-in-**ia** is a medical term;
- a defect of the dark African hole.
An Ethi (of) opia is near sightedness
of ethics, morals, and one's soul.

Who names these countries?
Who is playing God-mother?
Germanic Angles medical terms
for sure, not by any other.

What's in a name that ends the same;
a continent across the sea?
Ame.rica is rich of which is bitch;
as man, is one for me?

Af.rica for father? **Ame**.rica for mother?
The lands that bore the fruit,
will be dry as the many who die
are lambs of God to boot.

Why do all continents begin and end with letter A,
except for EUrope which is E?
Sounds good **eu**phoney! "Do good" **eu**baloney.
Eu.ro, then Asia 'ope' to be?

CaliforniA to PennsylvaniA;
States around the south ending in 'A'.
The 40th horizontal line, a dividing sign;
the Bible-Belt lambs of God to pay.

All the south-lands go down, and down means drown;
but believers rise, they pray and say.
If you believe in **Leaven** from Heaven,
there definitely is **no way**;

CaliforniA south to LouisianA,
to FloridA, to GeorgiA, then north.
To CarolinA and VirginiA;
To PennsylvaniA and so forth.

Unless you are fair and have the fare
when water fills the holes,
due to sucking energy from the land
to meet the capitalists goals.

The first to sink into the drink
will be a dark and sinful place.
One week of Mardi Gras booze,
and sex considered ace.

All the lower states in The Bible Belt,
are in the boat that's sure to sink.
Get a clue, heave.n (north),
and stay out of the drink.

If you leave.n and can eat the bread,
you will not rise; you will be dead
unless you own the boat right here on earth
and can capitalize on the virgin birth.

There's Hollywood, Dollywood,
Las Vegas, all the same.
But Carnaval and Mardi Gras
will mostly be to blame;

For unwanted bastards conceived
while worshiping the golden calf.
Sanctioned booze and beads, boobs and sex,
and all to get a big laugh.

Although I am thoroughly amazed
at how easy you've been to deceive,
and you keep on insisting boldly,
"ya-but, I really do believe!"

You'll awaken with a bang
when the land starts cracking and sinking,
and hope it's only a nightmare
from all that heavy sex and drinking.

Wonder why this is happening to you;
then realize it's your neighbors too?
Could this be it? Could 2000s be so,
when the sinners stay and the righteous go?

Heave.n up (north) toward the sun
where it's hot and bold,
instead of down (south)
where the lambs drown in the cold.

You Promised to Take Us Up There

Could it be you'll finally know whether or not
The Truth LIES in WORDS and you've been caught.
White lies are OK, white men say
Black lies are bad and we make you pay.

There was an earth cracking sound,
so I opened the door and looked all around.
A space shuttle was slowly lifting
from a secret hole in the ground.

Earthquake! Oh my God"! (I thought),
No, Dear **Jesus**! I almost forgot.
The ground was cracking with large holes in my lot.
The promises you made I believed, and totally bought.

I yelled and yelled as loud as I could,
but this shuttle was not made of wood.
A voice said "We told you it was for your own good
and you believed just like we knew you would."

"Ya-but, you promised to take us up there!"
"No-but", **they** said, "you haven't the fare."
You do have a choice; believe it or not.
You don't have to drown; don't buy the plot."

Puritan is fair; they're sure to get up there,
the Great White Brotherhood alone?
The fare is 'fair' but your cupboard is bare,
and diamond Jew-els you cannot own.

Ram that I am, religion is my name.
Ram Ewe for lambs, all part of man's game.
The meek shall inherit the dearth,
after man has dogged all it's worth.

Man will soon fly away with knowledge of this root race,
and return to earth someday, to again become the Ace.
The Ace is always in the pace, so it always starts slow;
Doling out bits-and-pieces to begin the earthly flow.

Rock n Roll in the 50s to begin a money-making phase,
Then Hoola-Hoop to Disco to start a new dancing craze.
The Earth spins faster ! Who cut the pie, disc-over-y?
In 2000s, a 6K Neros ends, and again many will die.

To be **born again** from out of this mother earth;
Out of Her water as an Amazon virgin birth?
Will **she** start life all over again
without the help of earth-bound men?

And so begins the contest of Oedipus Rex
with **He** who returns to earth to have sex
as is told "with the daughters of men,"
and rewrite the scriptures all over again.

So, ask me no questions, I'll tell you no lies.
Get down on your knees and pray for the prize.
You say you're a believer, in blind faith you trust.
Then stay on your knees and be**lie**ve if you must.

One day, you'll see that the big Eye lies!
Then, you'll be in for a big surprise!
Because Ewe are a sucker for THE WORD,
and Eye/Man used THE WORD to be heard!

Ewe/ woman say, Eye/man is a liar?
Eye/man say, Ewe/woman are on fire!
Ewe say, Eye am full of hot air?
Ewe and EYE, we make a hot pair!

Eye **see** the truth, then **tell** a white lie!
Ewe hear man's truth, then say "I could just die!"
Eye am the hole without a wife.
Ewe are the **w**hole, the womb of life.

Do you really need me now, having my genes?
Can you recycle; do you know what it means?
Will you make a boy, or an Amazon girl again?
I will be back, but only **who** knows when.

They tell us, "only God knows; He is in charge
of a boy or a girl, small or large".
But little by little you'll see a flicker of light,
about the truth in genetics held by the right.

A Yiddish **Oy** to the world! (a letter is missing)!
To B a worker Boy is a Jewish BLESSING?
A Portnoy's Complaint **boy** she wants and needs,
as she holds and counts her precious beads.

God/alien/man bestows on her a parthenogenic son.
Then, takes him back when his work is done.
HER pain is HIS gain - to rebuild the earth
After the "Who's Who" elite sucks out all its worth.

Karma, Dharma, reincarnation, then!
Each finds perfection; it comes down to when.

EGYPT BC

This story of Egypt began way back when
A young boy's father worshipped the evil God Aten.
His father Pharoah Akenaten who dictated sternly **what**
thou can see and hear, and what **thou shall not**.

"Aten is One" his father said, "a God you cannot see.
He is the only God and now that God is me."
His only son said "Re is God, Gods that you can see.
Ring-around-the-rosy Gods, the Gods of you and me."

"My Gods surround your God, see her around her Sun."
His father changed Re to Ra, and commanded it be done.
The son, a prince of peace when he was just a little boy,
pleaded with his father "stop the wars and help me
spread some joy."

The boy kept teaching love and peace; they hung him on a tree.
The seed, then planted by a little King (David) "a God
that you can see."
The Star of David; The Kingdom of Heaven on Earth;
will come from THE GREATEST STORY EVER SOLD,
about a Virgin birth.

The Roman **Pisos Family** wrote the script beginning A.D.
The Egyptian boy-King died while very young,
they hung him on a tree.
This King of the Jews will be crucified at the age of thirty three.
From virgin-birth to **Master**, to a martyred Christ superstar.
Arrange his birth for all it's worth and book three kings from afar.

We'll need the wisdom of their Sol.Om.On.
He is one who is highly trusted.
Then we'll add a man named Peter,
and friends Paul and Mary or we're busted.
We'll need priestly scribes, say..a Mathew,
a Luke, and definitely a Mark.
Baptist John will write his closest thoughts;
don't leave him in the dark.

John will preach "The Word is God", and we'll control The Word.
This Jewish man will claim he's "The Son of God"
and through him **we'll be heard**.
Of course, they'll claim "he's not our King," that will be the plan.
He'll insist he's "the son of God", and they'll say "Son of man."

Finally, a JewEl messiah; a savior seen as light.
From Moses the Old to Jesus the New; we've finally got it right.
Mythology to Theology, rewritten in the NEW literal sense,
will sell best in the West where they are metaphysically dense.

We'll need someone to claim his fame, and our man Saul
will sell it all.
Wait, we'll need a saint; we'll change his name to Paul.
Involution was, to evolution is, and that is understood.
Bad Saul was, to Saint Paul is, and the **Pauline System** will
be the good.

Think we can make Mary a believable virgin, a good Mother Earth?
We'll arrange for God to award her a son; a miracle virgin birth.
The Hebrews retold stories they took from the myths; I clearly remember ten.
Just count the many times they've done the deed, over and-over again,

That does it then, Paul travels to Rome, and he falls off his horse on his way
home.
It's important he ties the Old Testa to the New. We can't admit
Herstory came out of the blue.

"He is the messiah, the son of God" Paul will say in a shout.
We'll make Paul utmost believable and they'll buy it without a doubt.
If they tie this man's death to us, we'll deny it very, very loud.
The Jews will blame it on us Romans, and we will blame the crowd.

We must make it happen very soon, before once mighty Rome falls.
Even if the stupid people begin to think it's a giants' PAIR·A·BALLS.
Rome needs this script now, more than the Jews need Rome.
In 1948, the Jews will trade with the Angles for a place to call their home.

They have the Old scriptures. Paul and friends will write the New.
We, the **Pisos family** now have a superstar with miracles, and a great
cast and crew.
Rome will get to mass produce The Greatest Story Ever Told,
and best of all, Saint Paul will bring the Gentiles into the fold.

Holy Rome will spread our seed, east, west, north and south, indeed.
Martin Luther, a King not he; his Germanic words will come to be.
Angles will pro.test as planned; Confounding English words throughout the
land.
The time will come for us to be heard. The Word be God, and we own The
Word.

The author summarizes:

Could one seed three, or maybe ATEN?
Was Jesus the seed, or TWT ANKH AMEN?
King Tut and Akenaten with elongated heads;
Were they the ET Gods who could bring back the dead?

Let us go back again in time to Egypt and see,
how the seed of David really came to be.
From Pharaoh, to soldier-hero David,
then all the way to King of the Jews.

Was it the boy-King Twt.ankh.amen,
or a man they named Jesus who actually paid the dues?
Little King David, like Paul who was Saul
seeded a story called "I'll get you all".

Now it's the script-writer Steven, King of showbiz,
whose big screen theme is "I'll get you all for this."
Speilberg, King, and G. W. Bush, like David the Fox.
All of them are a genuine genetic paradox.

The cunning feline FOX is very Clever;
a Star of David died-in-the-wool 33/6 ever!
When the Fox is in charge of the chickens,
words of the tongue become slim pickins.

Time tricks from 33/6 who put the world in a fix.
They write it all HOW and we pay for it NOW!
Now the BIBLE has us by a PAIR·A·BALLS,
and theology gets high while mythology falls.

The Fox, an effeminate Dog rarely seen or heard,
would rather be a Cat, or better yet, a Bird.
To fly away from this pain-in-the-S called Mother-Earth
and return as the messiah by miracle virgin birth.

To return as **Jesus Christ Superstar,** a star that will not dim,
is greater than having a David star named after him.
To create The Kingdom of Heaven by birth,
and inherit The Kingdom of Heaven On Earth.

I see this clearly, an old story made new.
I may have been there, or possibly you.
Back, before this physical life in the past.
We all want to live forever; life everlast!

Re-write history, add the New Testa to the Old.
Add a name here and there, but follow the mold.
David, Sol.Om.On, MO.ses 10, and Jesus seeded,
all to be saviors at the time they are needed.

Likenesses of Pharaohs who fit the description
of old biblical characters, a deceptive depiction.
The time-factors don't jive that brought them alive,
unless you don't care, or blinded and simply unaware.

Plagiarism is a no-no even of a myth,
unless later you are privy to the FIFTH.
Mary and Jesus, Adam and Eve, Cain and Abel,
all form a Mytho-Theo-logical fable.

Change Abram to Abraham, Sarai to Sarah.
What just happened? Did you see what I saw?
From Shem to Sem, and Shemite to Semite.
Did you follow the H? It is now out-of-sight.

Sem is for semen, the seed we all can be.
Or **S**un, **E**arth, and **M**oon, three Gods that we can see.
Then there's **sem**inary, **sem**antics and **Sem**ite;
Aha! A play on words! The **Sem** is now in sight..ite!

Was Mo-ses Akenaten? Is Ra El from El Re?
Everything Code.X, a confounding language came to be.
The Hebrew Old and Roman New. Father, and Son
needs a Holy G-host, and three is made into one.

He says in the bible, "thou shall not steal",
although **He** didn't tell us, Africa'**S**pain Israel.
Don't read that stuff about numbers" **they** say.
"numbers do not lie; you'll find out one day."

I say, they say, and you ask, who are they?
The answer is "who's who"! They make you pay.
While having "Pie in the sky", those flocking birds.
Can't you see what I see? The truth **lies** in words.

See for yourself, a believer or not.
Most words are a **plan**, others a **plot**.
"In the beginning, **The WORD** was made man,
and women should ask; "a plot or a plan"?

Is it the truth, or are they very good acts?
The Pisos **New Testament** was written after the facts.
History, then **Her**story, one Old and one New.
A Pair-a-balls-from-Paradise; both from out of the blue.

His **from** the east and hers **for** the west.
Many wars are fought for which one is best.
Herstory is **present**, from **His**tory the **past**
The future will determine which one will last.

Aries the Ram before Pisces the Fish, for two.
But Aquarius will put them back into the blue.
With an Xmas present from the past,
and programs to **buy, buy**, and sell fast!

Saturn.day seven, or, a Sun.day-of-rest?
Warship the very one you believe is best?
Our God vs. their God; who is to say?
Did I say who, or who's who? It seems that way.

God is who.ever, what.ever, when, which and where.
I want to know **why**, but why.ever is not there.
Maybe finding out **how**.ever will fit,
but how becomes who, and **who's who** becomes it;
IN.HER.'IT'

ROME A.D.

The Roman Empire was dying to rule the mass.
They liked Paul's story of a good man on his ass.
Their Gods were losing their power of fear.
The masses needed a God they could see and hear
and relive a wondrous miracle happening each year.

They heard the New 'T' script about a **Jesus Christ Superstar,**
and three mystical kings who came from afar.
They recalled the words of the Old prophets who said
"The messiah will come back to save the dead."

These New "T" Pisos stories about this holy Jesus man
were very well written, but not by his hand.
The traveling salesman Saul / Paul, a disciple to be,
would tell the story as if this Christ were he.

One, about the "fisher of men" in all his glory,
who would feed the masses with a fish story.
The Romans would buy it and publish it all,
and no one would snitch that they bought it from Paul.

"It must be tied to the past, to the Testament of Old."
"Two Testis are better than one" Paul would be told.
"He is the messiah" Paul would say when from his horse he fell.
The Roman priest said "this man Jesus is a God we can sell."

"We'll have no need for soldiers" the Roman said;
"We have a God now who soon will be dead."
"The people will fall to their knees and pray,
VICARIUS PONTIUS FILEI DEI" (= 666)

"THE GREATEST STORY EVER TOLD
will be called **Her**story now that it is sold."
"A **fish story** you say, that it may be,
but now it belongs to The Holy See."

It begins with a woman who didn't have sex
with her husband. . . . . from Oedipus Rex.
"She will be God's mother and Jesus will be her son,
and He will be the God father: the Old Teste one."

"We'll give her an Ostrich, a bird born to fly!
We'll give him a choice, and he'll choose to die."
"He'll expose his ass with his **head in the sand.**
His Jawbone will crucify him **for the good of the land."**

"I like that" the Roman said, "as long as he stays dead".
Satersdag! Saturnalia! Mardi Gras! Carnival of Red!"
A Roman asked "will the tail of the dragon cut off our head?"
And the Pontiff said "not if the tail of the dragon is fed."

"Give them a Carnaval of revelry, **pie in the sky.**
The American Dream before they die."
"Whoever they are, they'll all wear a mask.
No-one will know or care, and no-one will ask."

"So, drink hearty men, get hot and make Mary.
Part.he.no.genes.is, for nine months she'll carry
A natural born follower, one of the flock.
A November Scorpio born under a rock."

"Afraid to be stepped on, they'll all wear the same mask
one year later, again, and no-one to blame."
Conceive near the head of the beast in the light,
Then, believe that your seed won't be lost in the night.

Who was that man who left her with child;
Plied her with drink and left her beguiled?
Do it by the numbers, all ye lads and lasses.
I call it "A Mess.Age For Them.asses."

Ezekiel said, "two, five, eight and eleven.
Follow the beast, it will lead you to heaven".
El Papa stood up, and demanded, "I'll be the Queen Bee!
God made all men workers, big busy-ness for me".

QUEEN BEE OF THE HOLI 'C'

The Roman Pisos family created a maleficent fib.
Much grander than the infamous Genesis 'rib'.
Good names needed to play the parts in a New Testament,
with all the script characters from Roman descent.

[New Testament characters]

How about a Mathew, Mark, Luke, and John as scribes?
Add a Peter Paul and Mary, and a Joseph to bring good vibes. With this many
characters, we'll need at least another "John". How about a John the Revelator,
John the Baptist, and so on.

Authors notes about the Pope

He is a feline man with the **habit** of a Cat
who covertly appears as a Fox;
The vicarious one called Holy Father
who is Papa to his flocks.
He is the Cat-holic Queen Bee of the Holy See
who the masses worship and pay the fee.

Have a habit, wear a habit, teach a habit "teaser."
From 3 a trinity, to 8 infinity, for Augustus Caesar.
She is a female kitty who doesn't have a name,
playing Virgin Mary has always been her game.

The male Cat's name is Tom "Tom hit-n-run".
Now **pussy**-cat has an unplanned passion son.
Tom doesn't beg like the subservient dog,
and doesn't get stuck! Just gets it done."

Female dog is the 'Queen B with an itch'
and she has a name, her name is bitch.
The male doggy has no name,
but he got stuck in the bitch just the same.

A virgin birth for the female cat;
A macho Tom-cat is where she's at.
Even though Tom didn't get stuck,
that black Cat ran out of luck.

To be, or not a worker Bee, for Papa and the Holy See.
Tom-cat had sex and now has to pay,
and prove once more that he's not gay.
Mama says, "you're no good without a wife.
You'll be a work-man-Jack for life".

But Jack jumped the candlesticks to get Jill;
He wasn't nimble; got burned, so up that hill!
Be a worker - man/Jack, a worker Bee,
and do it all for The Holy See.
Be a work-a-holic for the Queen. Outwork the Ants,
and get that green.

You'll be blessed within the hives.
The Queen Pope lives there and he wants lives.
Where did the Queen Bee get all his might?
The Holy Roman Empire won that fight.

The Roman soldier's "only enemy is love",
but he didn't get that word from above.
Now he's a macho Cat, programmed to be,
a busy.ness worker Bee for the Holy See.

The Queen Empress Dowager from the east
who seeded the concept of the beast;
Has her numbers - 666 R 18 sum to 9.
She was the world's most powerful fe-line.

She was known for one thing back then;
She made eunuchs of her servants – men.
She complains, "he's too small and thin as a rail,
and he's always chasing the bitches tail."

She says "castrate! Cut them off with my guarantee.
He'll get bigger, passive, and stay home with me."
The Queen Bee seems happy, but still wants more.
She acquired three big ones, and yet wants four.

"He's lazy" she bitches, "he acts like a jerk.
He's just like his father; that dog wouldn't work.
He had two big ones, then, he had none.
But now instead of two, I'll take only one."

"I'll put him in front and he'll think he's the best.
He'll have an EGO; from the east he'll go west."
Go west young man-dog; soon you'll get stuck.
You'll spot her naked behind and think it's good luck.

You'll go down from an 8 to a 3; cause 3 is more fun,
but then, you'll find out that 3 is two halves of 1.
Now, with only one testis, you'll try to prove two.
Your Old testis, plus the one you call New.

You'll lie like a dog about having just one.
But the one you call New belongs to my son.
You'll work like a dog, because a good doggy has two,
and gather some pesos and bring Papa a few.

One New Testis will make you seem odd,
but imagine, me, the mother of God!
Who will have more power; God, or his mother?
I am the Queen Bee, there is no other.

Yes, I am the Queen Bee and I am infallible!
You'll wear my number 666; it is indelible!
Three sixes are eighteen, a total of nine.
I am the Queen Bee of the holy FE.line".

I'll beat the Queen Ant someday you'll see,
and when I do, you'll all work for me.
I'll outlast the Protest.Ants, **His**tory is past.
Herstory is here now. The Old Testis won't last.

The New Testis is the ace in the pace.
The habit of the Cat will win the race.
Show me the biggest, toughest man in the west.
A macho American, he'll think he's the best.

Send him home where he has a wife to fulfill.
If she doesn't kick his ass, her mama will.
You tell me; who is tougher than mama in the west?
It's her mama, the toughest, and the best!

She kicks butt, squeezes balls and pulls noses with ease.
Castrato! Women's Lib. if you please!
And so, the Pope gives the teaching of the Empress with the itch
and becomes her 666 in time; "ain't that a bitch!"

ANGLES QUEEN PROTEST.ANT

The author speaks

The Cat-holic Queen Bee of the Holy See
and the Angles-Queen Protest-Ant, fighting to be
the Queen of all workers, all Jacks and Jills.
Queens get the money and "honey, you pay the bills."

Queen Protest-Ant labels Bee the great whore.
A pain in the pluralistic S, she always wants more.
First, a big one, cause bigger is more and better!
Create a pluralistic giant AmErica, utilizing one letter.

The Queen, played by Mary Shelley, speaks

"Worker Ants, go west, build 13 colonies for me
where the worker-bees get busy-ness for the Holy See.
Go and grow and experience the pain.
Work the native land and fetch me the grain."

"Mix with other dogs, cats, birds, and bees;
a pluralistic melting pot, if you please.
My dream is a giant! Part this and part that;
special huge parts with hardly any fat."

"I think of him as **AmErica**, a mother's dream come true.
A mixed blooded miracle, of red, white, and blue.
AmErica is a good boy inside, he'll do what I say.
Threaten the Queen and he'll make you pay."

"A pluralistic-giant, with parts he, she, and **it**.
A three-in-one mama's boy, assembled from a kit.
He/she/It was a dream creation, but I have a better plan.
I'll get a mad doctor to assemble it and blame it on a man."

"My virile young giant responds when I pull his string,
just like president Ronny, doing Nancy's thing.
He'll be afraid of nothing except hell-fire red,
and of course his British mama; my creation is not dead.

He is great at romance and good at song and dance,
and constantly trying to prove his manliness.
He flexes and groans, then burps and moans,
except when he wears that God-awful dress.

My boy scares the hell out of everyone,
then says "it's OK, I'm just having fun.
I'm losing my grip now that he's too big to hold.
And that thing with the dress is getting old.

I created a monster giant they all deride.
Soft inside is what he's trying to hide.
He wouldn't hurt a child or step on a flower;
my pluralistic sex-driven monster with all that power.

Look at him, AmErica, a God in the making!
But something went wrong, something he's faking.
They call him Satan, my giant bundle of joy?
Could they know my security/protector is not all boy?"

"He keeps mama well hidden; see what's first through the door.
Until I stretch his nose with anxiety, bronchitis, and more.
His constant pumping made **it** even larger than life.
I programmed him bigger is better, now ready for a wife.

I am his mama and I know what he likes best.
He likes to dream very big, so let him get his rest."
"Don't wake the sleeping giant;" Japan had it right.
When they did, my AmErica giant was ready to fight.

I told them "Whatever happens, don't let AmErica see red,
When he does, he roars to scare the dead."
I wanted to wake him when the Nazis struck.
But Mother England it seemed was out of luck.

Then, WW II happened! U. S. A miracle for Japan!
They hit him in his Pearl Harbor ass and that big boy ran.
First to the east, and he tamed that Nipponese beast.
Then, to Mama England's aid and the Nazis paid.

My giant got even bigger, with more muscle-power,
and became the keeper of the world, the man of the hour.
Now, he tells everyone how to be; where to go, and, what to see."
And yells "ya' ll are no good, unless ya'll are like me."

The Giant AmErica speaks

I am the biggest, and mama says I'm the very best.
So what if I'm an experiment, a Germanic pluralistic test.
It's all these 'Abby Normal' parts that make me feel odd.
On the inside, a girl, but on the outside, a mighty God.

Mama England tells me I Am **Eric**, a giant of a man,
but inside, I know I Am**Erica**, 'this-and-that' I am.
So I'll say it loud and clear "I AmErica right or wrong"!
In Texas, that'd be a dang good title for a song.

Japan taught us a lesson, "bigger is not better,"
but my ball and chain is that pluralistic letter.
I realize I'm a big pain-in-the-**S** called more,
but it's that Abby part that makes me a whore.

I know **what** I am, but I am searching for **who**.
"**Parts is parts**" but mine are red white and blue.
I realize I am big, but mama says I'm not all that bad,
and calling me **The Great Satan** makes me feel sad.

Face it, I've got this "**prove yourself**" hang-up driven by sex,
but mama never bothered to tell me about Oedipus Rex.
They say I've got more than I need and always want more.
Inside, I want all I can get but I know-not what for.

The boy in me wants toys, on this I'll agree,
but what is it in me that wants everything I see?
It's like, another person inside is kicking my ass;
saying "go fetch more toys if you expect to pass."

I am so big that I can take everything I see;
especially from anyone smaller than me.
I want people to like me, but what makes it tough
is when they say I should learn to share all this stuff.

I AmErica, and I'm very big and very proud,
but when I shout it out, they say I'm way too loud.
They keep on calling me "*the big ugly one.*
Tell me, what am I doing? What have I done?

I just want to be happy, just doing my thing,
but someone inside keeps pulling my string.
Melting pot pluralism isn't all it's cracked up to be;
programming people to want everything you see.

Being a giant Frankenstein monster is even worse,
with Mama England pulling my strings to fill her purse.

The author speaks

El Queen is.a.Beth has a castle called Beth El,
and Princess Diana said "her house was not a home".
There is a New Testament Angle for the Queens name,
Beth.el is that of Hebrew, but definitely not of Rome.

She would proclaim the King James Bible .
The Word of God from prophets old.
Then have **his**tory rewritten for the west,
and from that the creation myth was sold.

Now, out in the sand is a troubled piece of land
that is costing the Palestinians their souls.
The settlers move in and the Arabs pushed
out of their homes that now are nothing but holes.

We are told "One book to read, that's all you need",
and you must "In God we trust", even if you don't.
Believe it or not is basically what we've all got.
Some people believe, and now many won't.

The giant speaks

My Mother is the Queen of the Protest-ants.
I know she's the boss, because she wears the pants.
She is my 'other' and my mother; her dream I came to be.
So understand, most of this land can't work for the Holy See.

I live, work, eat, and sleep with the busy Bees,
but we each have a Queen and we're both on our knees.
When my Queen Ant kneads me, she pulls my string.
I stop what and who I'm doing and I do her thing.

You are a loyal puppy-dog, I'm sure that's what you say.
I say the bitch has power. She always gets her way.
She does call The Holy See "The great whore."
Face it, they both emasculate, they both want more.

So, if you're not nimble, and you're not quick;
You'll burn your ass on the candlesticks.
You too, will be a worker-ant or Bee,
and fetch for the Queens all that you can see.

The author summarizes

Adam, you ate the apple, now go to work.
Don't blame Jill, stop being a jerk.
She has her pain-in-the-S she must bear,
and the mark of Cain her son must wear.

She's insecure, so she uses man
to own her own Giant, that's her plan.
Dog/Man, you wanted sex and got stuck.
A giant puppy-dog, you're shit outa luck

I R EVOLUTIONARY

*Please take note that the letter 'I' in the title refers to the word **me**, and, the letter R should be construed as either **am** or **are**. As such, the title can be seen as "I AM EVOLUTIONARY", or "I REVOLUTIONARY". Also, note that the English definition of the three letter word **ire** is anger. Hence, Ireland is Land of Anger, and I know about Irish anger because it's the country of my mother's roots - Maxwell.*

*Many of the predictions I made since writing this poem in 1979 – which have come to pass thus far (2014) - are contained somewhere in the words of this historical (hysterical) "Riddles in Rhyme and Time" poem I composed during the out of body experiences I had, and since my fathers' funeral that year. One key prediction I made (in this poem) is the reference to: "Web and Net, scheme of things by man." I predicted in the 80s that the **Web** and (Inter) **Net** would come in the 90s based on the clue in the word-number Ni**net**ies.*

From and 8 to a 3, I R Evolutionary.
What goes up must come down,
The native ball soccered up and around.
Up from the east, West from the middle.
The CLU is NEW, an historical riddle.
Who cut the pie? Discover Y!
The Indian Gods; Sun, Earth, and Moon.
All must acknowledge very soon.

From an eight to a three, what was the fee?
The rape of the west as we all can see.
Three NEW fives are fifteen, a six!
Add one more for each country's fix.
Three sixes are eighteen, a nine!
Uncover the B and you will find
the Beast from the east, or,
parables from the pass-over feast?
U. S. A 'miracle' for the Japanese.
The Frankenstein Monster secured them a peace.
Eric and Isis, my.theology Greece.

From an eight to a three, the OM and the T.
Who kicks the bouncing ball, and
Who clips (eclipes) the sun?
Who "liberated" western Indian and left only one?
Who faulted the land and caused the Atlantic Ocean?
Who started the west hell-bent on 'E'motion,
to make Bible movies, mafia and war?
Please, dear God, we can't stand anymore.
Our native feet are weary and sore.

From an eight to a three, from a C to a D.
Thirteen! A four! The Dog from the Cat!
A cycle of nine, in.her.it is at.
Habit the odd Cat and see what you get.
Do not expect her home as a pet.
Curiosity is her name and Cat-holic is to blame.
But no matter, she knows the game.
The East tied her feet, first wok-n-woll.
Ten feet behind man with no balance or control.

From an eight to a three, who it will be.
In the middle, left is a five.
Nineteen hundred is evil, not live!
Odd - three, five, seven, and nine;
Cat is leaving Dog way behind.
Even – two, four, six, and eight,
"Who's who" do we appreciate!
Five and Ten is fifteen, a six!
Getting an ion to 'who' are the tricks!

From an eight to a three, what it will be.
Even or odd, Dog or Cat?
Odd Cat will be where it's at.
Is-o-dos - coming, exit the church,
Ten or eleven, tomboy the search.
Isis and Eric according to seven,
A six over five, 'It' is eleven.
It is go and motion; It is he/she,
Ego and Emotion, balance to be.
"Dog eat Dog", watch for the fowl,
fantasy Fox or maybe me-owl.
The wolf is an eight, and may be our fate

From an eight to a three, secret selfish the key.
Self is the flesh, and flesh is to hell;
Learn to sel-fish, you do very well.
First, sell the black and poor the white;
Then, take all their land and possessions in sight.
Give the native a bottle of booze.
He'll put on a mask made of cell-u-lose.
Suck from the earth and create a void.
Then tell the rest, I cell-u-loid!
Own everything the EYE can see.
Corporation Blues for you and me.

From an eight to a three, which will it be?
Father and daughter, or mother and son?
But why does it have to be either one
when doing it is really the fun.
Hir.O Hit.O, then soccer around.

She gives you asthma, Young Frankenstein sound.
She ties up your nose, It is mama, you see.
After all, daddy gave you to me.
Hell's frustration, Dog's nose out of gear,
the Company's got all the Cats by the ear.
The bird has the EYE, but the Eye Lies.
Follow the heart and be in for a surprise.

From an eight to a three, a nine equals me.
Young or old, woman or man?
Twas two-in-one China that started the plan.
Science? Religion? Need or greed?
Habit religion that planted the seed.
Humanity different or humanity same?
Is the feeling the number of name?
East, North, or West? We must know very soon,
before the cow jumps over the moon!

From an eight to a three, from a three to a nine,
man's evolution is a base-ball design!
The tail of the dragon will cut off the head
unless the tail of the Dragon is fed.
Eon to Ion, ever the pain,
the Indian pushed all over the plain.
Pain-in-the-S is pain we all feel;
Africa, Spain, Israel, Africa'S pain Is real!

From an eight to a three, why it will be?
Because EURO decides nothing is free.
What is at stake, a separate heaven?
"Who's who" to decide, a ten, or eleven;
first, we must reach a sensible seven.
I repeat, five and ten is fifteen, a six!
Getting ion to who are the tricks.
S.hellfish to all, cancer to be.
Keep the promise and not sel.fish to me.

From an eight to a three, where it will be?
In pace, or on earth? What is it worth?
Ocean emotion must be cut free,
Because time and space are not things you can see.
Matters not who's first in the race,
Considering the Ace in the pace.
No-body can be buried in a plan,
The lot is in the plot; Web and Net; Scheme of things by man.

From an eight to a three, when it will be?
Nineteen hundred to two, into the blue!
Including you, and me too?
Two is one and one, an eleven!

Accessory six, a fantasy heaven?
First in the eighties to stay alive,
frustration wars always start on a five!
Indian lands to determine the race,
Web and Net thrust in the **net**ies grabbing the space.

From an eight to a three, does it have to be me
telling the world it hurts being "so-called" free?
Destiny peace, or destiny fate?
We must do for others before it's too late.
Start with the western natives; balance the land.
Space shouldn't be such a drastic demand.
Need or greed? The truth, or a lie?
Does it depend on able to fly?
Or, is it a matter of able to buy!

A higher plane, or just better than you?
A just man, or, just who's who?
The "Who's who" are up there where
they cannot be seen by the masses today.
Controlling the world with religion, language and force,
not aware of the balance prophecy of **the 4th horse.**
I'm not completely sold that justice is cold.
If you and me strive to make it we,
then you won't hear I Revolutionary, I R Angry!

COLD MAN WITH A PLAN   2004

He came from the north **Ice** pole to control the world as his goal.
He was just a man, but with a cold "word plan", to call himself a **just** man.
He polarized using religion as his pol**ice** force while riding a white apocalyptic
horse. He was still just a man, but now with a very cold **Ice** Plan.

He rigged a cold, clever, language devise to call his evil plan **justice**.
Forcing boldly and prejudging coldly, he invented names to carry the blame.
Face of the **deep, dark, bad**, colo**red!**   "A better word" I'm sure you said.
With magic hands he rolls the d**ice**; appears the fixed trinity word Pre.jud.**ice!**

He selects only those able to speak a separate tongue, pose, and seek
To interpret his religion, medicine, and libel, from his **Dictionary** and **Holy
Bible**.

When the **Social Order** system was in, ignorance of the law was declared a sin.
Totally dependent on; looked up to in awe due to his l**ice**nse to pract**ice** law.
Down below them all the masses in the tail of the dragon passes, in sickness,
poverty, ignorance and pain, with very little chance however to gain.

The Queen says "Let them eat cake." They are too '*le miserabe* to feed;
to care for or save their seed. While on their knees paying the pr**ice** with very
little to suff**ice**.
Keep them out of a costly hospital to languish on the streets with l**ice**.

They are here to suffer and sacrif**ice**; to toil and sweat and pay the pr**ice**
until they are old and sick enough to die in a hosp**ice**.
"It should be the end" it has been said, one would assume when one is dead.
But just in case; "Omega, lend me a hand. Don't leave me speechless in the
sand."

My guides advise; "Go back to the beginning, to biblical man's tale of the
woman sinning. To Eden where **she** tempted **his** libido with the fruit of passion
and his almighty ego.
Go back to the woman Eve whom Adam in the Garden did deceive.
When He bit the apple twice and got thrown out of paradise.

Adam had two sons – Cain and Abel; enough to start a great fable. But, the
trinity plan needed a Seth; maybe a "to be or not" by Macbeth.
Man Jack, go back to the beginning; to cold man using her to **entice**; a taunting
woman in the plan. Knowing she tempts and puts testes in a vise, then keeps
on saying "Go to work and pay the price".

You'll find **she** was a ploy; a **plant** to make for you a boy. She was put there to
ent**ice** before the plan was all just**ice**. I ask: What kind of **ice** was used in this
cold plan we now know was conceived by man?
Cold **ice** isn't necessarily bad, unless it is **mal**, and that would be sad. **Mal.ice**
would surely be a **fore**-thought, but as an **Ice** plan, would it be bought?

You can bet on that to be **succeedent** Jack, and they won't take the **Ice Plan** back. Eye-man created the word and became God, and on Ewe, Eye will not spare the rod.

Eye-man have the world by the OLD and the NEW and no one can take it back Jack, not even you. Two books permuted and scribed for your fate. Two books that would eventually dictate; A mal word-plan made of evil **ice;** Two best sellers pre.scribed to cleverly suff**ice.**

By Romans, French and Greeks it was sought, and by Germanic angles re-scribed and bought. A confounding, pluralistic, universal language with very cold '**malice aforethought'.**

European collaboration as the illuminati wished. Permutation all through the age of the fish. A Germanic experiment, the seed was planted! Freedom of speech would be taken for granted.

AmErica, a Germanic pluralistic Frangk n'stein invention, of Anglo/European well-planned intention. Hebrew, German, Latin, French, and Greek; This confounding plural language took more than a week.

Phonics, semantics, prefixes and suffixes; nyms of homo, anto and euphonic mixes. Speak of a language made of ice, straight out of a "**Pair a Balls from Paradise**".

Eye/man knew she was a sucker for the word, so eye invented the word to be heard. I became God is the Word, The Word is God. An eye for an eye and don't spare the rod. But, The Word of God required another book, to dictate blind faith without a second look. The unquestioned Dictionary and the Holy Word. And an ET Fox behind the bush not seen or heard.

Two books from England and a game of 8 B all, with the Illuminati causing the meek to fall. The evil deity keeps the masses in control, but numbers now uncovered, will take its toll.

The "who's who" implies **Social Order** and Ice-men will now keep them across the border. **Social Control** is what the plan is really about and that you can bet on without a doubt.

Pol.**ice** and ent.**ice** keeps all men lurking, while 'prac**tice** makes perfect' keeps the masses working. Someday, someway, truth will endeavor, and people's lives will be in balance forever.

And so, the story of Just.**ice** is told about **A Cold Man With a Plan** who came from the North Ice Pole to control the world as his goal.

And now, **how** He does it with **words** from his dictionary and Holy Bible. Both are from **Eng.**land, and Eng is God; a three letter word, but don't think it's odd. After all, God is **The Word**, and **The Word** is God.

MAN'S DECEPTION

Composed in 1980

Adam and Eve, created to deceive the world through storytelling.
First came the rib, which begot the fib, but obviously very compelling.
She from He? Was it to be the first of man's deception?
He from She, my visions told me, but not from immaculate conception.

Letting man think He was to drink the juices from the forbidden.
Putting him first to ego his thirst, the plan was now well-hidden.
The law was now fact, libido intact; he cannot have **it** free.
He must fetch all his life to win him a wife, and surely pay the fee.

The system was in. Sex is a sin, unless it's for a kid.
Frustration in man was part of the plan, creation of the id.
He goes in front. His need is to hunt and he must show no fear.
In the east she stays behind, and soon he'll find her foot is in his rear.

He goes west thinking he's best, until he spots her behind.
She's now in front pulling the runt with his differential in a bind.
The motor that was pushing is now pulling as was planned.
Soon He will revert to being She, leaving mother earth un-manned.

REALITY - "A" Truth or THE Truth?   copyright 1980

A Truth is **A** Reality, controlled by the church.
The Truth is coming, now is the search.
The Truth is what is best for all;
The Christ-like jawbone taking the fall.

Program A Truth and system it well.
Em.ploy frustration; cancer the cell.
Is the rainbow real, or something you surmise?
To find that somewhere near the truth reality **lies?**

Is reality eye see, or reality I do? Is it "catch 22" controlling the Ewe?
The ic and the id, Monkey see, Monkey do. The Cat and Dog controlled by "who's who."
Liqu**ids** and flu**id**s flowing in all.   Creative ju**ic**es programmed to fall.
With accident babies running amuck, Advantages certainly not left to luck.

Faith in God, or faith in man?   Is there a difference, or part of a plan
to disengage from this earth, leaving the meek to in.her.it the dearth?
Space Arks are flying, the bird's in the air. "Ya but! You promised to take us up there!"
The truth from space, a voice loud and clear. "No but! We lied, you haven't the fare."

So, question Arks now before it's too late. Overt the truth, don't leave it to fate.
To think for ourselves, is it really a sin? When "who's who" lets no cats and dogs in.
Believing is painful for all Earth's creatures in sin, features for some, a new world to begin. Evolve to Revolve, is living the spin? We must stop the Revolver and let heart in.

CAPRICORN THE GOAT   Composed in 1982

God said "Capricorn the Goat is red, eat the apple and you're dead."
The Serpent said, "Surely you won't die". It told Eve the truth, it did not lie.
What **they** did was called a sin.   **She** enticed him and let him in.
Eve had a Kid, twas not a Lamb, from Satan the Goat, not from the Ram.

While raising Cain, they had another. A Lamb for God, Cain got a brother.
Like Cats and Dogs, the boys had a fight. Cain was **left,** and daddy's Abel right.
So, if red is **bad** and left is **wrong,**   and white is right – good and strong. Sing a
Kabalistic tune in a Sefirotic key,   But, what does it mean for you and me?

You worship Aten and call it a one. Satersdag is seven and one is the **sun.** Cain
is a nine and Seth is a seven. Ab.el eleven, the Lamb went to heaven.
RAM THAT I AM, the first month, now the fourth. Ewe give me lambs with
such remorse.   Eye am God, and Ewe are 'a sucker for the word'. Eye invented
The Word so that I would be heard.

Ewe are the soft ear and I am the almighty Eye. I programmed you to hear, even
though Eye lie. EYE AM THAT I AM; so, I am THE WORD of GOD.
And on Ewe – the ear, Eye won't spare the rod.
If truth be said, I AM 'THIS **and** THAT' I AM. Ewe are the sheep and I am the
Ram. RAM THAT I AM, Ewe will follow Eye. And, when Ewe are gone,
surely Eye will fly.

Back into space, where Eye started the **race** of humans, from the animals we
came to embrace. The true Gods are we, not He or She 'THAT' is **'in
question'**. "This and That" is to be!
Don't **Kid** yourself, give me a **Lamb** so that I can be all that I AM. A son that
will **be**gotten to carry my name. My insatiable libido and ego will bring me
fame.

If Ewe want all that Ewe are Abel to get, Ewe must listen to Eye to get in on the
bet. I am the all-seeing Eye of God on your green. The Bilderberg Illuminati
that cannot be seen.
Ewe are in blind faith and on your knees, and Eye can get away with anything I
please.   I've got you by the tongue; both eat and speak, and English will render
you ignorant and meek.

You live in our Langu.age of the tongue.   Speak **certain** words and you will be
hung. Jack points to those who are playing God over us and you must wise-up
without making a fuss.
Mind you, not everything is in that one book, There is much more knowledge if
you care to look.   Remember, **good** books are 'food for thought'. The book
that uncovers the plan, uncovers the plot.

THREE JACKS

JACK Be Nimble   JACK and the Beanstalk   JACK in the Box!

Jack was not nimble, Jack was not quick; He got his ass burned on the 'candlestick'. In the "candlestick church" Jack got a wife and began his fetch up the hill of life.
Jack knew that sooner or later he would fall, and lose his crown, but that's not all. Jill would surely make it a federal case, and Jack would have to find another place.

Now Jack's problem is not the ex-spouse, since he lost both his crown and the house. It's back home to mom who first kicked his butt, to get Jack "that dog" out of his lazy rut.
"Get a wife and kids Jack, and go to work or you'll end-up just like your dad, that jerk." Let's see, a good story for mom, Jack heard, that "all women are suckers for the word".

So, Jack tells mom he sold her cow for magic beans that grow somehow, high in the sky where he'll fetch home the Bacon.   Then, maybe mom will stop her belly-achin".
Jack knew the magic beans were just a ploy, to make him once more a mama's boy. It didn't last very long, that we all know, because those lousy beans began to grow.

Now Jack must climb and fetch a giant's bone, so he won't have to live alone.
Imagine! No wife, no work, kick back; watch TV, have a beer and a snack.
But Jack knows there is no giant in the sky, for if there was, there'd be no pie.
She's still mad about my selling the cow. "Go to work you bum!" I can hear it now.

Now mom's got her bone and still wants more. That means, Jack will soon be out the door. All Jack wants is a little fun and rest, but he'll keep hearing "mom knows best"."You're not lying around here drinking beer. Go look for a job! Get your lazy ass in gear." Jack searched all around but couldn't find a job. Jill had them all, so Jack decided to rob.

No money, no sex, and Jack couldn't fathom that, although he knew he could be an Army brat. He realized that once he started breaking locks, the system would put Jack in the Box.
For Jack, that dog, there's one-way out. The race for space, without a doubt.
Fly like a bird away from mother earth and let her have her virgin birth.

Jack/man will come back to earth again some day, to "have sex with the daughters of men" 'they say.' So, give the believers their wish; baptize the earth, and tell the lambs it is time for a Neros rebirth.
They all believe, and pray "the end of days is near." In time to come many space Jacks will re-appear. End of Jack/Man (on earth)

ADAM AND EVE

Composed in 1986

Adam and Eve created to deceive the world through storytelling.
First came the rib, which begot the fib, but obviously compelling.
She from He! Was it to be the first of man's deception?
He from She my visions told me, but not from Immaculate Conception.

Letting man think he was to drink the juices from the forbidden.
Putting him first because of his sex thirst, the Ice Plan was now well-hidden.
The law was in fact, his libido in tact, he cannot have sex free.
He must work all his life to win him a wife and surely pay the fee.

The system was in; sex is a sin, unless it's for a kid.
Frustration in man was part of the plan, creation of the Id.
He goes in front. His need is to hunt, and he must show no fear.
She stays behind, and someday he'll find HER FOOT IS IN HIS REAR.

TENN.IS.ANYONE?

Composed in 1986

Nine plus one is ten - is one. Ten is one. Tennis anyone?
Nine + two is eleven - is two. "9 - 11 is two, from out of the blue?"
Nine + three is twelve - is three. "Twelve is three, a spending-spree!"
Nine + four is thirteen - is four. "Thirteen is 'go four' and get more!"
Nine + five is fourteen - is five. "Five is jive, and brags I'm alive!"
Nine + six is fifteen - is six. "Yin Yang fix, since six plays tricks?"
Nine + seven is sixteen - is seven. "Nine and seven is closer to heaven.
Nine + eight is seventeen - is eight. "Nine and eight is not a good mate."
Nine + nine is eighteen - is nine!   "Nine plus nine gets along fine."
Nine + any number becomes that number. "with five, nine loses its **live**."
However! Nine **times** any number becomes nine!
"Nine times five is forty five - is nine. Nine is alive!
Nine plus ten is nineteen - is ten - is one. Nineteen is pain in the (letter) S!
Three in one!" Remember! Ten is one, and we are all one. So, TEN IS
ANYONE? TENNIS ANYONE?   IS **IT** A RACKET? **IT** IS ELEVEN.

AMERICAN RACE VS. A STEADY PACE
Composed in 2000 by Jack Tafoya

*This poem **AMERICAN RACE** is my way of indicating what America is*
***programmed to be** and **do** as compared to our main competitor from the east –*
*China. The question becomes: Who, **really**, will **win the race** in the long run;*
the rapid American Rabbit or the slow, steady, Chinese Tortoise?

The bite of a Beaver, a Kangaroo kick; **Doesn't** lay eggs, but f….ks very quick.

Rapid American Rabbit, bought its own story, then, lost the historic race
with a very slow Chinese Tortoise that kept a steady pace.

America! Chasing two rabbits could lose you **both** hares.
Chasing one at a time, you won't lose em in pairs.

Make it a habit to chase one rabbit until it stops for a rest.
Ultimate speed is not what you need. You'll find a steady pace best.

The ace is in the **pace,** and a steady pace wins the race!

THE YOU AND THE I   Composed in 1982

In the beginning there were two, the I and the You .
The You said to the I "it is thee I wish to be."
And in response the I said, "if You think it, You be;
For from a thought grew a tree."

"A tree, a marvel" said the You to the I,
"surely It is a wonder, not I."
The I spoke to the You and said, "again
tis a wonder You seek; I will make men"

Said the You to the I, "a man shall I be
so I may be mighty and brave as the sea."
The I made a man straight as a tree.
Borrowed the peace and calm from the sea.

The man grew in size strong and erect.
He said to the I "what have you done?"
The I said "I have made me a son."
"A son," said the man; "is that what I be?"

"I wish to be brave as the sea."
"You are," said the I; "brave as can be.
Bright as the sun, for joy I have made.
You are my son."

"Something is missing" the man said to the I.
"Trees are planted in soil, the sun's in the sky.
The sea travels a distance, a path I do not know.
Tell me from here, where do I go?"

"You go the distance, as surely as I,
You are as much as the sea, tree or sun in the sky."
"You are I, and I can be whatever you think
is needed of thee, be the sea, tree, or sun,

 For when You are, WE ARE ONE!"

PERSONAL POETRY

*I spent time in New York's Rikers Island in 1982 on trial fighting a charge of possession of Coca that I was set-up for (isn't that what they all say) while I was in N.Y.C. in 1977, but I cannot complain.   The time I spent in Rikers was one of the best two-year **learning** periods I spent, involved in doing research for my books, although these Personal Poems – unlike my Historical Poetry - were never intended to be in a book. But, here they are!*

*The first poem – **LOCK IN**! – portrays the frustration I went through attempting to deal with the chaos and racket my eyes, ears, and brain had to withstand - mostly during the day, when the cells were open and all the dogs (even numbered birth-dates) were barking and chasing cats (odd numbers), like Protestants chasing Catholics. ...and here I was, a bird trying to stay above it all. This was a time (1980s) when teen-age Hip- Hop was taking hold and Rap (then Black music) was first being explored. Being a jazz person and into metaphysics, the activities and excruciating sounds were very painful to my sensitive ears.   I must admit, I am a snob when it comes to the arts, especially music. In short, I feel the same about music as I do about women – "If I can't have what I really want and appreciate, I'd rather have none".*

My genetic code number (7) makes my eyes and ears very sensitive. Loud, repetitious music drives me crazy. Likewise, I simply cannot appreciate a woman who dresses loud and/or talks (raps) repetitiously and says nothing. The voice and anatomy are precious commodities. This is probably why I have an aversion to loud, repetitious Rap music today, although many of my friends have told me my Historical Poetry should be done by a Rap artist to reach young people. LOCK IN portrays my frustration in endeavoring to endure the mental pain of being locked in with human animals.

LOCK-IN !

Composed while on Riker's Island 1982

A bird! An Ostrich! Am I not to fly, to once again feel the cool breeze of expression? Tied by a passion to rebellious caged cats and dogs, locked on an island of inhumanity, spreading insanity.

Existing with thieves, killers, pushers, and pimps in chaos, frustration, and pent-up aggression. Seeking from me a magic of wisdom for tomorrows, to make their painful past and present disappear.

So many ingenious self-taught legal minds encased in the flesh of drop-outs, trying to reinvest in a future far-off, yet near; Looking to me for their own discarded answers.

Speakers blaring! TV glaring! Shouting over the din. Showers splashing! Iron gates crashing,   while smoke keeps filling the air, and I hear repeatedly "does someone have a cigarette to spare"?   There must be a quiet place somewhere.

The harsh sounds of pain, cruelty, and ignorance rings in my head while justice prevails, and these overcrowded jails overbalance the scales for those who are fortunate, but not willing to share; except for spending more and more funding on jails that claim to slow recidivism, but miserably fails.

It's killing my ears, pounding my head; my heart is feeling the pain. Dear God, if I could only hear soft music again. It's all way too loud! I can't think! My ears are in hell! Then, with groans and moans I hear the gates slam.
Finally! LOCK- IN! I lay back alone in peace for a spell.
Are my ears still working? I actually hear a mouse lurking.
The noise that I hated is somewhat abated; It is now much better in here.

Lock-up my flesh and try to system my mind; then find, that killing my ears leaves only my eyes, the institutional fee. But, if I end up like all the rest, they'll get no help from me.

My ears are linked to my heart, as seeing is mostly a lie! If I can protect my ears for a few more years; Again, I will fly and enter my castle in the sky. Till then, I will exist in this cat and 'dog-eat-dog' PEN called RIKERS, the New York penal island of unruly men.

The next poem I wrote after my mother passed away in 1983 while I was in
Rikers. It tells the story of my conception, birth, and perceptions while growing
up with my mother and trying to comprehend and understand her, let alone
being one of twelve children, me being the 7th, and, following in my fathers'
footsteps playing jazz music and being an artist. My mother ostracized my
father when I was a teenager and turned the family against him, especially the
boys that she needed for her longevity.

EARTH MOTHER

To my departed mother

New Years Day 1983 from Rykers Island.

You gave me being, you gave me life.   You brought me back into this world of
strife. You caught my spirit returning to earth. You called me "stubborn right
from birth."

I hung on "breach", not wanting out. Of peace on earth I had great doubt.
I didn't want to face the sorrow and pain of coming back to this world again.
"A mind of his own" you always said when speaking of my searching head.
You called me "different' from the rest", always putting you to the test.

Watching, testing you and perceiving; learning and yearning but always leaving.
I lived my life away from home, doing for others, but always alone.
Coming back seldom to stay in touch, realizing I wasn't wanted that much.
I knew I was different than the rest; you whispered secretly "you are the best."

You couldn't tell me what to do even though I came out of you, asking who,
what, when, where, and why so many people must suffer till they die.
I yearned for love and found it naught in human kindness, which I sought.

Now you are gone and we're all alone, and I can't even call you on the
telephone. There are many things I wanted to say, but the way things were,
there was no way.

Even though our words were few, in your heart you really knew.
And now that you are up above, you can see that there was love.
Like dad, I know you will talk to me from where you are and hear my plea.

Please listen now and remember back, when and why you named me Jack.
From my father you begot, me, a man of spirit and of thought.
The seventh born, the son of man; My late father told me of the plan.

You alone weep on my search-path seven left me by my father now in El.even.
He touched me with messages from above saying how painful it was without
family love.

41

I lost my family also, but with destiny as my new start;
"Following in my father's footsteps" with music and with art.
I heard his voice and I obeyed; certain of what he said,
"Jack, it's all in the numbers;" It wasn't something I read.

"Look into the future by going into your past; Family genetics, names and places; numbers ever-last. The answers to the number codes the people desperately need, are hidden in your past-life; find them, then proceed."

I found the answers after many years of constant search. I found that most are hidden within the Mormon Church. Now I am a threat "to those who hid the secrets well, and became the "Holy Empire" when the Romans fell.

Earth Mother, you know my heart and why I am back here. In this earthly time and space, I was to reappear, to reveal an urgent mess.age that will soon up-rise, revealing "within our present truth, physical reality **LIES.**

You grant me the compassion to forgive, and the fortitude to teach and live in this world of sorrow, anguish, and pain, to help make it balanced and whole again.

You are the Earth Mother from whence I came, and left; and returned to be tested again. Involved in the flesh for routine inspection. Devolved, then evolved to spiritual perfection.

I've given years of my life to the spirit of man, but I have learned there is a much greater plan. Doing for others we can all eventually find a way to the Kingdom of Heaven on Earth someday.

The time draws near for me to leave this place and join with my 'guides' somewhere in space. 2014 will bring us into an inhumane religious war and catastrophic water waves that will say "no more"!

I have lived in these probable end of days to bring forth truth and balance in many ways. In 2022 my earthly world of pain will cease, and we can finally be together in peace.

See you soon, Your son Jack

YOU ARE IN THE MOMENT

The next poem was sent to me from a young lady named ROXY I learned to appreciate, who at age 20 did not know she was 'bi' until I made her consciously aware of it, and purposely introduced her to another 'bi' female (friend Sally) who wrote and sent the poem **DEAR FRIEND JOAQUIN** *following this one. Both ladies are poets.*

To Jack Tafoya in Rykers Island 1982

My love, yours was the face I saw this early morning.
When, watching my glance in the mirror en-route to dreaming of you.

A collage of memories played like favorite old movies cross the reflection of my minds eye, when all at once, the past succumbed.

And the timeless satellite shot forward to now, right now. And I sent my warm blood across to mingle awhile with yours.

As I rolled my hands within the faucet's stream of warmth, my eyes still fixed on me and you, I knew that all is as we chose (and we laughed.)

YOU ARE IN THE MOMENT, not of it, Jack. Not everyone can claim this. More than ever, I notice "free" men are victimized and miserable, (while your mind grows pearls in RYKERS clamped shell.)

Love, Roxy

DEAR FRIEND JOAQUIN

In Rykers Island 1983

My friend Sally sent me this next poem from Portland Oregon. Her brief writing gives one insight into her perception of our friendship and my situation in Rykers.

First, I found your name In a letter postmarked Portland.
Alongside birth-dates and equations A new seeing structure, another eye.
And I tinkered with the toy. Tried on judgments for size.

Now I think tools don't need judgments - If a hammer won't turn a screw;
Don't use it.

In three days in your house You were more with us than with your plight.
Inside a vicious cold, the renaissance of a nicotine vice, your heated swimming bed and Ram Dass from your bookshelf.

In this fourth encounter scene, I found you my eye-level friend,
My walking companion On a pliable path.

I leave my hand in yours for you, No matter if we mold our roads to forks. And

so will I carry the eye you've shared with me.
These gifts from which the giver gains Weigh lightest on the path. And won't
be left behind,

Love, Sally

EVERYTIME I LOVE YOU

From Rikers Island 1982

*I penned the next poem **(tongue in cheek)** to my friend Roxy almost jokingly -
as you will notice - and followed with **NOTE TO A LOVED ONE**.   I found
that I enjoyed writing poetic **letters**, especially in the form of "Rhythm in
Rhyme."*

Thinking back, I do remember, it was sometime in November.
After talking we were glancing; fortunately I asked you dancing.
I teased with "jazz is on tonight." You smiled saying   "jazz is out of sight."
After dancing, we had fun, and later on we came as one.

Now I lay here thinking back, we were quick to hit the sack.
I'm not usually so fast, because I've learned it doesn't last.
But, somehow fate kept us together through those months of lousy weather.
And every time we'd have a fight, making love was dynamite.

Like falling off a cliff, I screamed, cause each and every time, it seemed;
That when I'd whack you from behind, the cat in you is what I'd find.
Now, every time I lie in bed, I try to see you in my head.
I close my eyes and picture you, and concentrate on someway new.

I'd taste a breast between my lips and fondle one with fingertips.
And, when I'd feel you wanting me, I'd enter you in ecstasy!
Then, just when you were wanting more, someone always banged the door.
I'd search for you, but you were gone, and I realized the 'system' really won!

Next time, please stay with me a little longer, then my picture will be stronger.
And when a prison guard bangs the gate, luckily he'll be too late.
Worse than flashing lights above you, it happens EVERYTIME I LOVE YOU.

Let's hang on baby past the sounds, until ecstasy abounds. If the bottom of the
cliff is near, maybe I will find it here. I'd rather find it there with you and keep
on searching till I do. When I find it, I will know that our thoughts have made it
so.

I will stay if you will too, and make it happen EVERYTIME I LOVE YOU.

Peace and Love,   Jack

CHRISTMAS NOTE TO A LOVED ONE

In Rykers Island 1983

*The next poem to Roxy portrays my general feelings about the over-all sadness at Christmas time, but even more-so in jail. "Those who can **give** at Christmas time are happy, while those who can't....and this is the **minority** masses [actually the majority] who have nothing, are unhappy.*

How sad it was when Christmas past, I thought I'd hear from you at last.
The mailman came, went, and came. A couple of cards without your name.
From my lawyer, and my sister - two! Mom; I really needed to hear from you.
Of all the times one shouldn't be sad, at Christmas time, it's really bad.

Being sad, but not surprised, I thought of you and then surmised
that maybe you no longer cared, even after all we shared.
No word for two months, almost three! I count the days as you can see.
I finally called but you had gone way out west to Washington.

The last time I heard from you was good. I asked "please write;" You said you
would. Caring a lot is bad enough, but missing you is really rough.
We both have needs, feelings, and pride, and there are things we cannot hide
from each other in our heart, even-though we're miles apart.

I'm man enough to understand other matters in demand.
I realize you've other things to do than think of me the whole day through.
I sit here writing and I ponder, does absence make the heart grow fonder?
The feeling is either there or it is not.   One cannot **make** it cold or hot.

I know the joy. I know the pain. I swore I'd never care this much again.
An injured heart I've had before. Not the same, but maybe more.
I guess what I'm trying to say, on this most sad and miserable day; I'm just
feeling helpless and alone, and trying not to use the telephone.

Wow! There's a phone-call for me now! It's as if you knew somehow.
I'm so relieved, you're still alive. And, your Christmas letter just arrived!
I'll end this rhyme and read it now, and mail this silly poem anyhow.
Not hearing from you for so long made me feel something was wrong.

I just didn't want to ass-u-me. I tried to leave you plenty room.
But now I know it wouldn't last; we made it happen way too fast.
I somehow always knew that you were 'bi', and our 'thing' was bound to die.
But loving you was well-worth the time, and everything has turned out fine.

Sincerely,   Jack

SO BE 'IT' ROXANNE

In Rykers Island 1983

This poem I wrote from Rykers attempting to open-up Roxy to the fact that she was 'bi' long before she realized it and finally experienced it as a phenomenon just before turning twenty one. I had the advantage of knowing her genetic code numbers (10), a highly evolved unisex potential (like an ET)! I have since come to a controversial conclusion that "all women are bi-sexual by nature" but are not allowed (by man's laws) to explore it. After all, we are finally coming to terms with "we are all ONE in nature". The strange fact is that I am "straight", but have spent many years in NYC working and associating with, and learning to understand the sexual revolution from a woman's point of view. The two books I wrote go into detail about my time in NYC during the battle for the ERA and the ticker tape marches by the gay women and gay men fighting for their rights.

When you were just a little boy in daddy's dreams of years gone by.
Your mommy planned you more than he, an **IT** 'to be or not to be.'
Growing pains are such a bother when a girl thinks like her father.

Pulled to one side, then the other, but you'll be just like your mother.
Adolescence! Throw the ball! Soon he'd have you do it all.
But he left, and then another step-dad moved in with your mother.

Teens! A dress! A little bra! Now you can forget to study law.
Be a girl a while and dream of love, cause little boys are push and shove.
June is bringing you to twenty. Find a man who'll give you plenty,
room to be or not to be; Both, boy and girl, just wait and see.

Now's the time, your 'growing year.' Think of me and you will hear, me sending
Happy Birthday from my heart, even-though we're far apart.
My feelings grow stronger with the pain, thinking we will re-unite again. And,
while they have Jack in The Box, I'll dream of you and get my Rox!

Your best friend, Jack

A SUMMER AFFAIR

The next poem is a song I wrote about my experience with my soon-to-be Dutch wife from Aruba, Netherlands Antilles in 1962. I performed it for the first time on stage in Aruba while Tina and her parents were in the audience. As it turned out, it wasn't just A Summer Affair.

Yesterday last summer, when the world was mine. We were so in love that we kissed while we poured the wine.

Yesterday last summer, seems that I recall, You did something strange; tears and mist while we kissed and my heart took a fall.

People say you flirt a lot. Was it just a game? Something tells me you played the game right from the start, but, now you need me, don't let us part.

Please say you love me. Show me that you care. I'll remember you and I'll know that it's not, just A SUMMER AFFAIR.

MY CHILDREN

In New York City 1978

MY CHILDREN (by genetic code numbers) is a very brief peer into my perceptions of what went into my childrens' individual conceptions and manifestations.

5 seeds sown on sympathy's ground.

The 1st - active sprout, possibly unknown – Michael - 5

The 2nd - like a bird, alien, travelling alone – Patrick - 11

The 3rd - bred a wolf/dog barking. - Larry - 8

The 4th - struggling, blooms the sensitive Fox - Jeff - 6

The 5th - a passion conceived weed of hypnotic beauty - Laura 3

Lies the planter's pain of five seeds sown.

THE WIZZARD OF OOZE NYC 1976

Dedicated to friend Timothy Leary

The next poem is a tongue-in-cheek concept of my experiential time in NYC in the 70s with some controversial famous people who experimented with hallucinogenic drugs i.e. LSD, Peyote, etc.   They labeled me The Wizard of Ooze due to my ability to comprehend and function while under the influence. I did this with famous professors and Psychologists of that time.

Time snapping fingers beat, spaces oozing creams;

Sweet creams, loves creams. Whipped creams tasting life.

Life's times spaces beats. Enjoys it, tastes it, sucks it, loves it.

Only spaces fingers beat. Love, whipped and creamed.

LOVE (or whatever) POEMS

composed in my teens

1. BEEN LOVED NOT

2. WARMTH OF YOUR SMILE

3. I'D RATHER GO BLIND

4. MY WHOLE REASON FOR LIVING

BEEN LOVED NOT   AGE 13

The first cut is always the deepest.
With every beat, a little more of me is lost.
Although in time, the wound becomes unseen,
Only the scar in my mind could reveal my true cost.

The best buy is not always the cheapest.
With every look I reflect upon my actual worth.
Although in time they say it just becomes a dream,

The last goodbye is always the hardest.
With every memory the tears are all that I've got.
Although in time, I will learn to accept what is real,
that I have loved and been loved not.

WARMTH OF YOUR SMILE   AGE 18

Beneath the stars that shimmer to the story of your eyes
and the presence of your lovliness in the open skies
I walked along the beach, dreaming of song and laughter,
letting the rushing waves touch me with sighs and feeling
the warmth your smile has brought to me for the days coming after.

I just walked for hours, waiting for the Sun
when the the journey I am making has begun.
I can't refuse the feelings coming through my heart,
cause every happy ending needs to have a happy start.

I'D RATHER GO BLIND   AGE 15

I'd ride through the heavens
on my white Stallion masted in 'sevens'.
Dressed in Purple Satin and trimmed in a scarlet haze,
Collecting clusters of Stars
And arranging them in moonlight bouquets;
To give to you, just to say "hi".

I'd ride through some high windblown cliff
as twilight falls, and crimson splashes in the sky
and evening melts into night.
Through the restive walk in shadowed pathways
that spill upon the sand,
I found the light to give to you
just to let you know I care.

I'd ride through some peaceful country lane
on my imaginary buckboard,
brimmed with fields of summer grain.
Daydreaming of a tide that is slowly turning
washing all my heartaches away,
but only if you become a part of the fire that is burning.
Can I give you the seeds of my love, to let you know
that it only needs time to grow.
And, from the seeds of summer grain come another day
to give to you, just to say
"I'd rather go blind that to see you walk away.

MY WHOLE REASON FOR LIVING   AGE 14

A little bird chirping merrily a love song
in the peaceful and tranquil night,
stops to let a few gentile raindrops
moisten his delicate wings.
As he bathes, I see his shadow
distant in the moonlight.
And beautiful thoughts of you
are close as he sings.

My thoughts are of a new world
the paradise that you've given me,
where raindrops fall in the mystic colors of a rainbow
though just for a while.
Cause the rainbow curled around my shoulder
to let me see the Sun's rays
and the music of an Angel's Harp
intertwine with your smile.

Where the trees glitter with Emeralds of green
and the velvety grass contains the perfume of trust.
Where the little animals nibble at your feet
as soon as you were seen,
and the Gods ruled love, peace and harmony as a must.

Where the flowers have encircled my head
as a crown for the part,
for I am being treated and feel as though
I were a King.
Where the relationship I have with you,
whether for one moment or forever,
I shall cherish it with all my heart.
Where without you my whole reason for living
could not sing.

METANUMERSYLLOGY - Definitions

WHAT DOES METANUMERSYLLOGY MEAN? WHERE DOES IT COME FROM?

META-NUMER-SYLLOGY IS A NEW 3 PART (PLURAL) WORD CONSTRUCTED BY THE AUTHOR JACK TAFOYA TO COMBINE THREE SEPARATE LANGUAGE STUDY ENTITIES. IT IS THE METHOD HE USES TO 'READ" AND ADVISE PEOPLE. IT INCORPORATES THE ELEMENTS OF NUMEROLOGY AND ASTROLOGY BUT IS MORE ADVANCED AS IT UTILIZES SYLLOGISM - *LOGIC AND REASONING -* WHICH INCORPORATES SCIENCE.

META – *A prefix meaning changed, transformed, as in* **metamorphosis. Note! And higher, as in Metaphysics.** *Meta is mind and physics is body.*

NUMER - l. NUMERUS, A NUMBER; + LOGY (LOGIC) - NUMEROLOGY *a system of occultism involving divination by numbers* (NUMER – from number.)

SYLLOGY – From SYLLOGISM – *Fr. L. Gr. (syn – together, plus logizesthai, to reason, logic) a form of reasoning in which two statements or premises are made and a logical conclusion drawn from them. Example; All mammals are warm-blooded (major premise); whales are mammals, (minor premise): therefore, whales are warm-blooded (conclusion), 2. Reasoning from the general to the particular.*

LOGY – Gr. *Logic – science of correct reasoning, valid thought or deduction etc. Specific kind of science, doctrine.*

LOGIC – Gr. Logos, word, speech, thought. 1.*The science of correct reasoning dealing with the criteria of valid thought. 2. Correct reasoning, valid induction or deduction. 3. Way of reasoning. 4. Necessary connection or outcome, as of events.*

METAPHYSICS – After the 'physics' of Aristotle. *The branch of philosophy that deals with first principles and seeks to explain the origin of first principles and the structure of the world. Speculative philosophy in general. Abstract or obstruse.* Meta – *mind,* physic – *body.*

PHILOSOPHY – FROM PHILO AND SOPHY. PHILO – *Gr. Loving, liking, having a predilection for, as in Philo***logy. Logic of Philo.** SOPHY – **Sophist, sophism – Fr. L.Gr. A wise man, a learned person. Any person practicing clever specious reasoning. Specious – (appearance) seeming to be good, sound.**

PHILOGYNY – Philo, *Love for,* gyne, *a woman.*

THEO – *Gr. A God, or God, (the)*

THEOLOGY – *Study of; the logic of God.*

THEOSOPHY - *Study, (clever, specious) reasoning of God. Love of God.*

IDEO – *Fr.ideo - *Gr. Idea, a combining form meaning idea, as in ideology. – the study of ideas. A way of thinking.*

IDEOLOGY (I'di-ol-e-ji, id'I-) n. (see ideo and logy) the study of ideas, their nature and source. 2 Thinking of an idealistic abstract, or impracti cal nature. 3. The doctrines, opinions, or way of thinking of an individual class, etc. *specified kind of science, doctrine.* The logic of ideas?

NOTE! Id – L. it) In psychoanalysis, that part of the psyche which is the source of instinctive energy dominated by the pleasure principal and impulsive wishing; of "ego", "superego", the "self".

EGO   e'go, (L. egos) 1. The self, the individual as aware of himself. 2. In psychoanalysis, that part of the psyche which consciously controls the impulses of the id", of superego.   Note   the   numerological   significance:
I D – E – O – LOGY
9 4   5   6   3677
1 3   9 14
 4 + 5 + 6   5
        "6"   "5" = "11" master number

RELIGION – *Fr. Re-, back (again) plus legare – to bind. Any specific system of belief, worship etc. often involving a code of ethics, as the Christian religion. A state of mind or way of life,* Note! *Exact, conscientiously, as – he worked with religious care. Cleanliness was a religion to him (habit)?*

THE WORD RELIGION (LIKE METANUMERSYLLOGY) IS A PLURAL WORD FORMED FROM THREE ASPECTS 1. RELI.   2. G.   3. ION. The prefix **reli** is the same as rely as shown below. The letter G represents the **force (G force)** which is the mother figure in the trinity. **Ion** represents infinity or future. Together meaning: RELY ON THE FORCE (G) FOR INFINITY. **RELI - G – ION.** THE FIRST MONTH OF THE ZODIAC (OUR FOURTH MONTH) IS ARIES THE **RAM – THE FORCE (G) – RELIGION. RAM THAT I AM!** LETTERS I AND R HAVE THE SAME NUMERICAL VALUE – 9, THE FEMININE NUMBER. HENCE, "I AM (THIS AND) **THAT I AM."**

RELY – (reli) [OFr. L. *religare; see RELIGION], to trust, depend, have confidence (with or upon).*

NOTE! THE LOGIC OF RELIGION = RELI (rely on) G (the force, mother for) ION (INFINITY. Hence, rely on mother for the future. She will demand you go to work and bring the 'bacon' home (security).

CODE – Fr. L. codex, tree trunk, etc. 1. *A body of laws (numbers?) of a nation, state, arranged systematically for easy reference. 2. Any set of principles, as, a moral code. 3. A set of signals for sending messages, as by telegraph, flags etc. 4. Note! A system of secret writing in which 'letters', figures (numbers) etc. are given special meanings, (coded, coding), to put in a code; translate into the symbols of a code.*

DE.CODE – *To translate (something written in code) into comprehensible language – de-cod'er. "I am the decoder." Joseph and the Pharoh.*

You will find this and much more in my books found at www.jacktafoya.com

Printed in the United States
By Bookmasters